D1759911

THE
TIMEWARP
TRIALS

WILLIAM
THE CONQUEROR
GUILTY OR INNOCENT?

Stewart Ross
illustrated by Élisabeth Eudes-Pascal

ReadZone Books Limited

First published in this edition 2017

© copyright in the text Stewart Ross 2011
© copyright in this edition ReadZone Books 2017

First published 2011 by Evans Brothers Ltd

The right of the Author to be identified as the Author of this work
has been asserted by the Author in accordance with the Copyright,
Designs and Patents Act 1988.

Printed in Malta by Melita Press

ISBN 978-1-78322-636-8

Visit our website: www.readzonebooks.com

THE TIMEWARP TRIALS

WILLIAM THE CONQUEROR

GUILTY OR INNOCENT?

Stewart Ross

illustrated by Élisabeth Eudes-Pascal

Defendant

DOCK

Judge,
The Honourable
Ms Winifred Wigmore

CLERK
Mr George S. Cribble

Prosecuting lawyer,
Miss Tankia Bessant

PUBLIC GALLERY/PRESS

The High Court of History

Witness

WITNESS BOX

JURY

Defence lawyer,
Mr Leroy Williams

In the beginning...

THE FOURTH PERSON Professor Horatio Geekmeister brought back from the dead was inspired by a birthday present. It came from his grandson Charlie, carefully wrapped in tissue paper inside a cardboard box. The professor unwrapped the gift and put it on the table before him.

A mug. A white china coffee mug decorated with a picture. Geekmeister picked it up and looked carefully at the image. It showed three men sitting rather awkwardly under a sort of awning. The margins above and below the main image were filled with birds and a rather fat dragony thing.

Over the shoulders of the important-looking man in the middle, who was dressed in a red robe and carried a sword over his left shoulder, were seven capital letters. With a gap in the middle for his head to poke through, they read: WIL – head – LELM. Ignoring the head, that was WILLELM.

The professor recognised it immediately. It was a picture from the famous tapestry showing the events of 1066: the year of the Battle of Hastings, the last time England

had been conquered. And the man who had invaded was the man on the mug, William the Conqueror.

Geekmeister leapt to his feet with a squeal of delight. That was it! There was the person he would bring back to stand trial. William the Conqueror, hero or villain?

As always when he needed advice on his re-creations, the professor met with his great friend Doctor David Gibbon, the famous historian.

Yes, David agreed, William the Conqueror would be a fascinating person to put on trial, but there was a serious problem.

'Yes?' The professor looked agitated.

'The usual business, Horatio. Getting hold of some of the Conqueror's DNA. His tomb was wrecked, twice. The second time, over 200 years ago, they found just one thigh bone inside. Then even that disappeared.'

An anxious look descended over the professor's lined face. 'Vanished completely?'

David frowned. 'Well, local people said it was put back in the tomb under the floor of St Stephen's Church in Caen, France–'

'So we will take it out again!' interrupted the professor.

'Unlikely,' said David, shaking his head. 'The church won't let you. Lots of people have asked and the answer is always "no".'

'"Never take no for an answer" is my motto,' said the professor grimly. 'I'll find a way.'

It wasn't easy.

Geekmeister's many inventions – a way of generating electricity from water without any pollution, for example – had made him fabulously wealthy. Some said he was the richest person on the planet. He didn't show off this money on unimportant things like cars and clothes, as some people do, but spent most of it on research.

Money had spoiled the professor in one way, though. He had come to believe that he could buy anything he wanted. Normally this was true. But when it came to the priest in charge of St Stephen's Church, Caen, he was wrong.

Mais non, the man insisted politely, the professor might not open the tomb of William the Conqueror. His remains should be left in peace. No, not even for a million pounds would he change his mind.

That was that.

But it wasn't, of course. Not long after the priest had rejected Geekmeister's request, about two hundred metres from the church, a large house with a garden came up for sale. Someone bought it and moved in with a number of men and women in overalls and hard hats.

Two months later, Professor Geekmeister called his friend David. 'Got it!'

'Got what, Horatio?'

'DNA of William the Conqueror, of course. Now I can set about bringing him back to life for the trial.'

'But you weren't allowed into the church. How did you manage…?'

'Don't ask, David. It's secret. I'll give you just one clue: read a book called *The Wooden Horse*.'

Doctor David Gibbon bought a second-hand copy and sat down to read. It was about prisoners of war escaping by digging a tunnel….

Ah! thought David to himself. So that's how he did it, the old fox! He tunnelled under the church and entered the tomb from below.

The Accused

FOUR CHILDREN sat on the jury of the High Court of History. Each time the court met, a famous man or woman from the past was brought before it and accused of a crime. Together with the eight adult jurors, the children had to decide whether the accused person was guilty or not guilty of the charge against them. Professor Geekmeister had insisted on having some children on the jury because he said that they were much better judges of character than adults.

'Can't wait for this one,' said Tom, who had been on the jury with his friend Jasmine for the three previous trials. 'Haven't the foggiest what this William the Conker is like.'

'Conqueror,' corrected Jasmine. 'He's not on a piece of string, you know.'

'But he might be round and hard and—'

'Silence! Silence in court!' The voice of the court sergeant, Victor Vanwall, rolled round the court like an approaching avalanche. 'Please stand for the judge, The Honourable Ms Winifred Wigmore!'

Rising to their feet, the jury, the officials, the media workers and the members of the public in the galleries watched as Ms Wigmore walked slowly to her seat, picked up her papers, arranged them neatly, and sat down.

Everyone else resumed their seats and waited eagerly for the trial to begin. Above them, the TV cameras rolled, carrying the extraordinary drama live to every country in the world – except one. The country that banned the programme was ruled by a king who thought it would not be a good idea to show a king on trial. It might give his people ideas.

'Ladies, gentlemen and children,' began
Ms Wigmore, 'we are assembled here today to
hear the case of a famous man. He is accused of
theft – of stealing nothing less than the crown of
England. And when we say "crown", we do not
just mean a round metal hat that lets the rain in–'

She stopped and glared around her. Someone
in the public gallery had dared to snigger at
her little joke.

'Remove that person from this court!'
snapped the judge. 'Now!'

She pointed towards a plump lady in a flowery frock. Two security guards swooped and escorted the scarlet-faced giggler through the door.

'We will not allow the dignity of our court to be mocked,' Ms Wigmore explained. 'Let that be a warning.'

She glanced down at her notes. 'When we say William of Normandy is accused of stealing the crown of England, we mean he stole the entire kingdom. He removed the existing king and took all power for himself.

'It is the task of our jury to hear the evidence and decide whether William stole the crown or simply won it in a fair fight.'

Ms Wigmore turned to the jury. 'Is that clear?'

'Yes, My Lady,' said the foreman of the jury, half rising as he spoke.

'Very good. Call the defendant!'

'Certainly, My Lady!' The court sergeant braced his powerful shoulders and marched out of the courtroom, followed by his two security officers.

Jasmine turned to Tom. 'Now we'll see whether you're right,' she whispered. 'Bet he's not round and hard.'

'You're on! Bet you a chocolate bar at lunch time.'

'Right.'

The pair shook hands, making sure they were out of the sight of the judge's beady eye.

Just a few moments later, the sergeant's heavy footsteps could be heard marching down the corridor leading to the courtroom. Victor Vanwall strode into the room. Behind him, walking upright with a strong, springy step, came a tall, thin man with brown hair, cut short.

Jasmine smiled to herself. The man's face looked just like that in the tapestry: sharp blue eyes set like glass beads in a shapeless lump of mozzarella cheese. She scribbled *conker??* on a piece of paper and slid it over to Tom. He glanced down at it, added, *You wait!* and passed it back to Jasmine.

'Would you tell the court your name, sir?' asked the judge when the defendant had taken his place in the dock.

'William, by the grace of Almighty God, King of England and Duke of Normandy.' The voice was hard and grating.

'Thank you. Now, sir, do you know the charge against you?'

'Charge?'

'Before I answer that,' said Ms Wigmore, 'I would ask you to show a little more respect to this court. You may have noticed that I call you "sir". I would appreciate it if you used the correct title when addressing me.'

William said nothing.

'Well, sir?' said Ms Wigmore after a long and awkward pause.

William's mouth remained tightly shut. For almost three minutes, the judge and the accused stared at each other. Neither blinked.

Eventually, William said slowly, 'So you want me to play your game….'

Still the judge did not move.

'My Lady?'

Ms Wigmore finally relaxed back into her chair. 'Ah! That's better. Thank you, sir. Yes, I do want you to play my "game", as you call it. But I promise you it is no game.

This is very real, sir. This is the High Court of History.'

She paused a moment for her words to sink in. 'So, sir, you understand the charge against you?'

'Yes, My Lady. Some ignorant fool says I stole the crown of England.'

'Precisely. And how do you plead?'

'I don't plead anything, My Lady. I am no thief, nor ever was one. The crown of England came to me from God Almighty and the will of King Edward.'

'That is for my court to decide, sir,' the judge replied. 'I take it, then, that you plead "not guilty"?'

'Indeed!'

Judge Wigmore nodded and jotted something down on the pad in front of her. She then ran over their duties with the jury, reminded the public gallery to keep quiet, and invited the prosecution to begin its case.

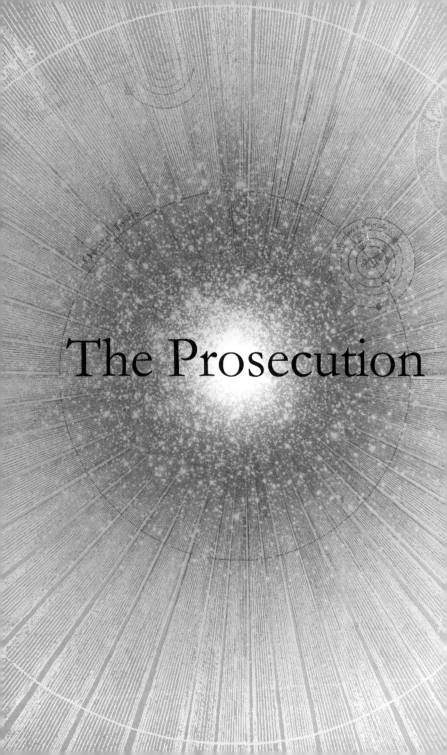

The Prosecution

TANKIA BESSANT, the lawyer for the prosecution, was not one to hang about. As soon as she had permission to begin, she rose, bowed to the judge and walked over to stand before the jury. She then did something neither Tom nor Jasmine had ever seen before. She smiled. Beneath her raven hair and hook nose her mouth opened to reveal two perfect rows of gleaming white teeth. They were so white and so perfect that Jasmine was sure they must have been straightened and polished by a dentist.

She was smiling, she explained, because she had never had such an easy case to prove. The jury would find it simple to reach a guilty verdict, too, she said. She smiled again. They deserved an easy case after the difficult trials of Henry VIII, Guy Fawkes and Boudicca.

Why was it easy? Because it was obvious that William of Normandy had taken what did not belong to him. He had done that sort of thing all his life, often with great cruelty. Miss Bessant offered an example. In around the year 1052, William attacked and captured the French town of Alençon.

He liked capturing towns because it made him richer and much more powerful. Unfortunately for the poor folk of Alençon, they had managed to annoy the Duke of Normandy in some way; so, when he had captured their town, he ordered the defenders' hands and feet to be cut off.

'That, respected members of the jury, is the sort of man we're dealing with. Steal a crown? Why, he'd steal his own mother's purse if he could get his hands on it–'

'Enough!' roared William. 'I will not stand here and listen to that foul woman pouring venomous lies and abuse into people's ears. If I were back in my own time, I would do a great deal more to her than just cut off her hands and feet! I'd have her tongue sliced out and–'

It was now Judge Wigmore's turn to interrupt. After getting William to calm down, she turned to the prosecution lawyer.

'Miss Bessant?'

'Yes, My Lady?'

'Please remember that you are here to prove a case against the defendant, not to be rude to him. Please take back what you have said.'

Tankia Bessant looked rather shocked, but she did what the judge said and apologised to William before continuing with her speech.

'As I was saying, the defendant was a conqueror. He conquered Alençon and, before he turned his attention to England, he conquered the French county of Maine. He even had a go at Brittany, an even larger area of France.

'He was a greedy man, greedy for land, greedy for power, greedy for money. But what he wanted most of all was a crown. He wanted to be a king.'

Miss Bessant swung around on a single high heel, sending her hair swirling like a cloak behind her. She walked quickly over to stand before the defendant.

'I was going to call you simply "Your Grace", as that is the correct way to address a duke. But since you did actually become king of England, I will call you "sire". Is that alright with you, sire?'

William said nothing.

'Very well, sire,' the prosecutor went 'on'. 'I will take your silence for a "yes". Now, by what right did you claim the throne of England, sire?'

William looked at the judge.

'Yes,' Ms Wigmore explained, 'you have to answer these questions, sir.'

'I will then. The crown of England came to me through the will of God and the hand of King Edward.'

'King Edward?'

'I believe you know him as Edward the Confessor. He left his crown to me.'

'Ah! Thank you, sire.'

Ms Bessant walked away a few paces, as if she was thinking. Turning back to the defendant, she asked, 'Let us take the first point. Why do you say God gave you the crown? Would you explain, please?'

It was very simple, said William. The Pope had blessed his army and God had allowed it to win the battle at Senlac Hill, the fight in which King Harold had been killed.

Ms Bessant explained to the jury that Senlac Hill was where the Battle of Hastings had taken place. She then asked William whether God had allowed Harold to become king before him.

'Of course. Maybe he was punishing the English people for not living good lives. He gave them a bad king to teach them a lesson.'

Ms Bessant let out a little whoop, as if she had just scored a goal. Spinning on her heel again, she marched over to the jury.

'You hear that, ladies, gentlemen and children?' She was almost shouting now. Tom and Jasmine had never seen her so lively.

'This man says God may have given King Harold to England as a punishment. Ha! I tell you, it is far more likely that God gave England that man–' she jabbed a finger towards the defendant – 'as a punishment. That monster who cut off hands and feet, who killed every man, woman and child in the north of England to teach them a lesson.

'No, honourable members of the jury, God did not give the crown to William I. He stole it. By force from the man whom the people of England had chosen to lead them, King Harold.'

William's white face was trembling at the attack. Jasmine looked at him carefully, trying to work out whether it was out of anger or fear. She couldn't tell.

By this time, Prosecutor Bessant had moved back to the dock.

'Then you say that King Edward the Confessor left his crown to you?'

'That is what I said. I didn't realise you had forgotten. Perhaps your memory is not quite sharp enough for this job?'

Tankia Bessant's head jerked upright. 'I beg your pardon, sire?'

William's lips spread in a thin smile. 'Oh, did I upset you? Just paying you back for some of the things you said just now.'

'Paying back? Sire, I did not think that you had much of a case before this trial began, and now–'

'Miss Bessant!' cut in Judge Wigmore.

'Will you please stop trading insults with the defendant and get on with the case?' She was clearly annoyed at having to calm things down a second time.

It was turning out to be a much fierier trial than anyone had been expecting.

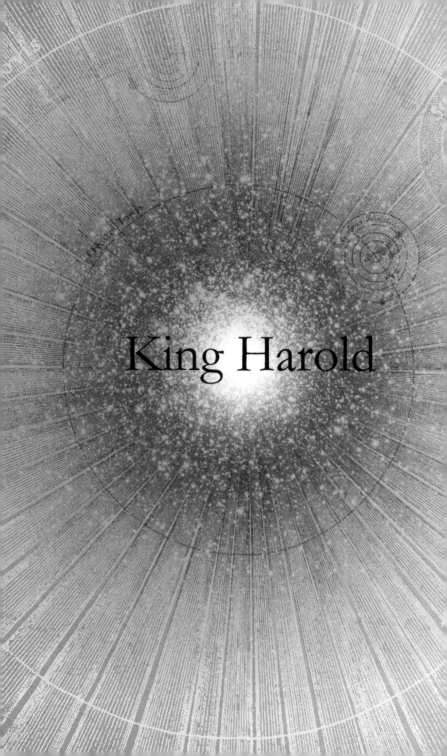

King Harold

AT LUNCH TIME JASMINE AND TOM
very nearly had a row about who had won the
bet. Tom said William had a round face and
hard eyes, so he was hard and round like a
conker. Jasmine said he looked a bit flabby, so
he certainly wasn't hard. He wasn't round, either,
but quite tall and muscly.

In the end, the argument was solved by
one of the other children who offered to
buy them both a chocolate bar to celebrate
his grandma's birthday. He didn't mention the
fact that the day itself had actually been two
weeks before.

In the afternoon, Prosecutor Bessant
called for her witness to be brought into the
court. No one knew who this would be, as
Professor Geekmeister had kept their
identity a secret. There was a general gasp
of amazement, therefore, when Miss Bessant
invited King Harold II of England to enter
the witness box.

Needless to say, the first thing everyone
looked at was Harold's eyes. They were
disappointed – not a hint of an arrow wound
anywhere. The professor had recreated Harold

not as he had been at the time of his death, but a couple of years before.

The Anglo-Saxon king was a truly impressive figure. Tall and strong with long fair hair and a droopy 1970s-style moustache, in his flowing clothes he looked a bit like someone attending one of the first Glastonbury Festivals. He sounded a bit like it, too, with a slight Wessex accent in his rumbling voice. (Another of the professor's little tricks.) Jasmine was not the only young lady in the room who thought he was rather attractive, in a quaint sort of way.

'Thank you so much for coming here, sire,' Tankia Bessant began, sounding a good deal less aggressive than she had been with William.

'My pleasure, madam,' replied Harold with a smile. 'Actually, I didn't have much choice in the matter. One moment I was in great pain, holding my eye and thinking what a fool I had been to look up in the middle of battle, and the next I was lying on a table in a laboratory with all kinds of wires sticking out of me. Odd feeling, really.'

'I'm sure it was, sire. But let's get down to business. First of all, do you recognise that man over there?' She pointed to the dock.

William's eyes narrowed.

'Good heavens!' exclaimed Harold. 'You here too, William? You scoundrel, I gather you nicked the crown after I had gone, is that right?'

'You were the one who stole it, Harold Godwineson,' said William coldly. 'And you got what you deserved!'

'Liar! You always were a tricky–'

'Gentlemen!' interrupted Judge Wigmore, slapping her hand on her desk. 'You are here to answer questions, not to ask them. And certainly not to engage in a personal slanging match. Is that clear?'

While William simply nodded, Harold apologised to the judge most sincerely. Was that just a hint of a smile she gave him in return?

Prosecutor Bessant resumed her questioning. 'There are two things I would like to know, sire. First, did you swear an oath to William that you would help him get the English throne? Second, did the dying King Edward and the people of England choose you as their king?'

The court waited in silence to hear what the last Anglo-Saxon monarch had to say. His answers held the key to the whole case.

'I could lie to you,' began Harold, 'but that is not my way. The answer to both your questions is "yes"!'

There were gasps of astonishment in the public gallery. Even Tankia Bessant seemed thrown for a second.

'Are you telling the court, sire,' she said, 'that you swore to help William get the throne of England – and then took that throne for yourself?'

That is precisely what happened, he said. But he needed to explain. In the year 1064, before he was king, and simply Harold Godwineson, Earl of Wessex, he went across the Channel on royal business. He was captured by Guy, Count of Ponthieu, and held prisoner. Ponthieu was part of Normandy, and when William heard about this, he immediately told Guy to hand Harold over, which he did.

'So it was,' Harold explained, 'that I became the guest of that man over there.' He nodded towards William. 'Guest? Ha! He treated me well, yes. But would he let me go? No, he would not. Not until I had sworn an oath to help him take the crown of England on Edward's death.

'It was a vile trick. I was trapped. What could I do? Remain a prisoner all my life in some stinking Norman castle – and probably be murdered there in the end – or swear this wretched oath?'

Harold turned towards the jury, staring straight at Jasmine. She blushed deeply and looked away.

'Yes, members of the jury,' Harold went on, 'I took that oath and William released me. That's how he got the Pope to support his invasion of England. He told the Pope I was an oath-breaker, a terrible sinner.

'But the moment I arrived back home, I went straight to a priest and explained what had happened. He said that a forced oath is not valid. A true oath must be sworn freely. I prayed to God, therefore, and my sin was forgiven.'

Answering more questions, Harold said that the Archbishop of York knew about the forced oath. That is why he had crowned Harold as the

true king of England in Westminster Abbey. And blessed him, too. He would never have done that to a sinner.

Harold's answer to the second question was easier to give. Certainly, the dying King Edward had asked Harold to take over as king of England. The whole of the royal court knew this, and no one objected. The nobles, the bishops, the scholars and other wise citizens of England – everyone had accepted Harold as the true king.

'There you have it!' said Miss Bessant when her witness had finished. 'Now you have the truth. Harold was the rightful king and that man over there, the man in the dock of the High Court of History, is a thief!'

'There is no doubt, is there?' the prosecutor concluded as she walked over to the jury. William had forced an oath from Harold and used it to trick the Pope. The Duke of Normandy had no real claim to the throne of England. He seized the crown by getting together a band of thieves and rogues and promising them English land and riches if they helped him win his crown.

Many joined William's army – the world is full of adventurers – and, as luck would have it, they killed Harold at Hastings, and the Duke had his evil way. He became a king.

'And that, My Lady and honourable members of the jury, brings my side of the case to an end. William, Duke of Normandy, William the Conqueror, is and always was a vile thief!'

Miss Bessant spoke so powerfully, so harshly that she sounded a bit like a bully, thought Tom. Whatever his mind said, in his heart he could not help feeling just a little bit sorry for Duke William.

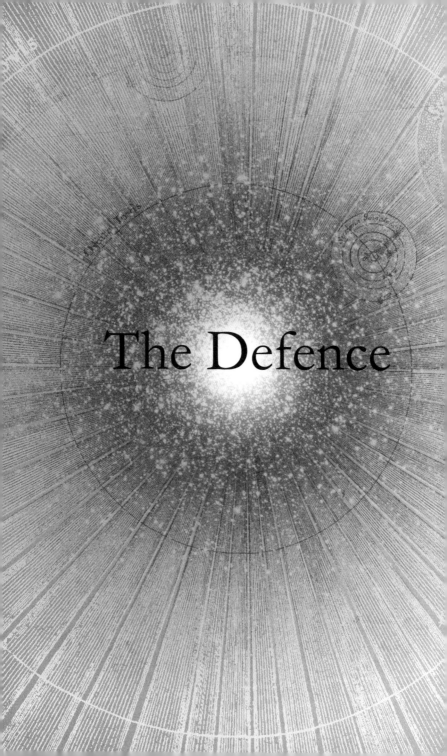

The Defence

'RUBBISH!' said Jasmine when she heard what Tom thought about Duke William. 'How can you feel sorry for a creep like that?'

Sitting about in their special room during a meal break, the children in the jury were discussing what they had just heard.

'He's not a creep!' Tom frowned. 'I bet you'd try to be a queen if someone gave you half a chance!'

'Maybe I would; maybe I wouldn't. That's not the point, Tom. I still think he is a creep – all that sneaky oath stuff!'

'That's the way they did things in those days, that's all,' said Tom, trying to keep calm. 'You don't like William because he killed Handsome Harold, that's what it's really all about!'

Now it was Jasmine's turn to get het up. 'You don't know what you're talking about, Tom Walker!'

'Yes I do, Jazzy!'

'And don't call me Jazzy! My name's Jasmine!'

Once again, the situation was saved by one of the other children. If Tom and Jasmine didn't calm down, the sensible Year Sixer explained, they'd never be asked back on the jury. Anyway, they'd been told not to make up their minds before they had listened to both sides of the case. They hadn't heard a word from the defence lawyer yet.

'All right,' muttered Jasmine. 'Leroy'd better be good to change my mind, though.'

He was good, although whether he was good enough to change Jasmine's mind remains to be seen.

In his usual manner, Leroy Williams began his defence by strolling over to the jury and smiling. 'Ladies, gentlemen and children – we must not forget the children – you have heard a powerful attack on the defendant, King William. Indeed, I must congratulate Miss Bessant on putting forward such a strong case. Quite something, wasn't it?'

Mr Williams paused and shook his head. 'Sadly, though, Miss Bessant forgot to mention some key things. Or perhaps she left them out deliberately?'

Jasmine leaned forward. She wanted to know what defence of William there could possibly be. He looked so evil, for a start.

'Let's begin with a little history lesson,' the defence lawyer said, walking slowly back to the centre of the court. 'When a king or queen dies, who takes over their crown?'

The question was so like school that Tom only just stopped himself from putting his hand up.

'Well, we all know what happens nowadays. In Britain, anyway, it's the eldest child who inherits the crown. In Saudi Arabia, however, the job is taken over by a brother. So it's not the same everywhere.

'Back in the eleventh century – the time of King Edward the Confessor, Harold and William here – it was never so clear who should inherit the crown. King Cnut, better known as King Canute, got his crown by conquering England. He was followed by his two sons. The second one had the odd-sounding name Harthacnut.

'When Harthacnut lay dying, he left his crown to a man he wasn't related to. You know who that was? No? Well, I'll tell you: it was Edward the Confessor.

'Yes, Edward the Confessor became King of England after the previous king left him the crown. A sort of dying gift.

'Once, perhaps twice, Edward left the throne to the man in the dock, William the Conqueror. Just as Edward had been left the same crown. Can you now blame William for coming to claim what had been given to him? No, of course not! William is no thief. He was simply coming to take what Edward the Confessor had promised him. It was his inheritance.

'Does that make him guilty? No, it does not. He was only doing what everyone else would have done.

'And even if Edward had not left him the crown, he still could have taken it. Cnut, one of the country's greatest monarchs, seized the crown by conquest. Why couldn't William do the same? And he believed his successful conquest was God's way of giving His approval. Maybe we don't all think that way today, but it doesn't mean it was wrong. Just different.'

Leroy Williams was such a charmer and he explained everything so carefully that Jasmine was now really confused. It was fascinating, too, better than anything they did at school! Why couldn't all history lessons be like this?

The defence lawyer was now standing in front of the dock, looking straight at the Conqueror. 'You are a deeply religious man, aren't you sire?' Mr Williams asked.

'You know the answer to that question. During my first life I placed all my trust in God my Saviour. I built two fine abbeys and gave much gold to many churches. As a king and a duke, I had great power; but my strength was but a tiny ripple before the storm of God's might.' The words were spoken with such force that when William finished the court sat in total silence for a moment.

'Thank you, sire. And when Earl Harold came to visit you in Normandy, he swore on holy bones to help you to the throne of England?'

'He did, yes.'

'Was it wrong of him to break this oath?'

'Wrong? It was a terrible, terrible sin for which he will be punished in hell by torment too awful to describe.'

Mr Williams looked down. 'The poor man!' he muttered.

'Poor man?' said William, flaring with sudden anger. 'No, he is not to be pitied. He knew what he was doing – and he will pay the punishment in hell!'

The lawyer nodded, thanked William for his answers and turned back to the jury. It was now obvious, he suggested, that William was an honest, deeply religious man. Yes, he was an ambitious one, too, but that was no crime. He simply took a crown that he believed should be his.

There was one further point to be made before he called his witness, Mr Williams explained. If the crown of England was to stay in the same royal family, as it does today, then neither William nor Harold should have had it. There was another man. His name was Edgar the Atheling, a descendant of Alfred the Great.

'This Edgar was in England at the time of the Battle of Hastings,' Mr Williams said. 'In fact, when they heard of Harold's death, the people of London proclaimed Edgar to be their new king.

'They changed their mind when William and his army arrived, of course. Edgar then made peace with William and the two got on reasonably well for the rest of William's life.

'So what does all this show? First, there were no hard and fast rules for who should inherit a crown. Second, William, an honest man, really believed the crown should have come to him, not Harold. He arrived in England not to steal it but to claim it. That is why the Pope supported him. That is why so many soldiers came to his side. He was, you see, in the right.'

Jasmine now had no idea what to think. Tom, too, was a bit bewildered. Leroy Williams made it all sound so simple. Yet there was no getting away from the fact that the English people had chosen Harold, not William. The Duke of Normandy was a conqueror who waded to the crown across a river of blood. Harold, on the other hand, had picked it up amid cheers and prayers. Peacefully.

Which one, if either, was the thief? What a knotty problem!

The voice of the lawyer cut through the children's thoughts. 'And now, to prove William's innocence once and for all, I would like to call my witness. Please bring in King Edward the Confessor!'

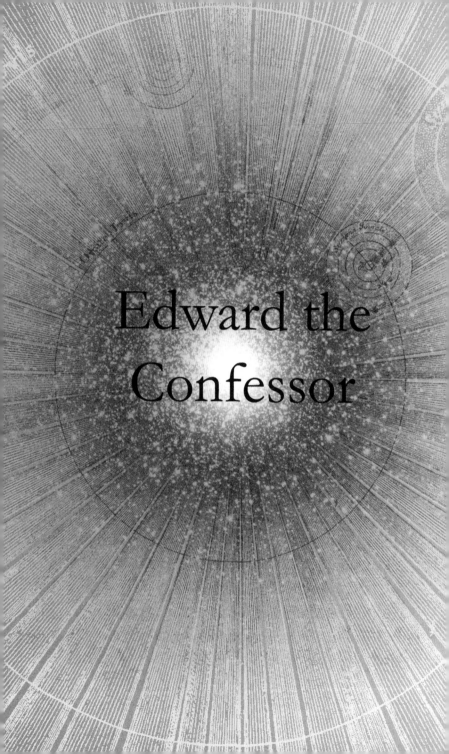

Edward the Confessor

NEITHER JASMINE NOR TOM were quite sure what a "confessor" was. Tom thought it was something to do with being especially religious, a person who apologised a lot for their sins. When he mentioned this to Jasmine, she asked whether this was because Edward had loads of sins. Tom didn't know.

They weren't too sure when Edward appeared, either – although he certainly didn't look like someone who might have done a lot of wicked things. The man who shuffled slowly into the court was elderly, with white hair and a rather straggly beard. Jasmine wondered, rather naughtily, why Professor Geekmeister had given new life to someone who would enjoy so little of it before he departed again.

'You are, sire, King Edward of England?' Leroy Williams asked with his usual smile.

The king blinked and peered around him. 'Yes, well, I suppose I am,' he said in a quavering, somewhat squeaky voice. 'And this really is a bit of a surprise. Fancy being here now! Well, well!'

'Well, well indeed,' said the defence lawyer, hoping that his witness did not rabbit on too much. 'With permission, sire, I would like to ask you a question.'

'Of course.'

'Thank you. Would you tell the court whether you offered the crown of England to anyone to wear after your death?'

'Well, let me see. Did I offer...? Well, yes, now I come to think of it, I did.'

'Thank you, sire. Now, would you kindly tell the court who that person was?'

The question caused a sudden change in Edward. His eyes narrowed, one hand tightened on the dock in front of him, the other twisted anxiously in the folds of his flowing robe.

Ah! thought Jasmine. Not quite the dear old thing you first seemed, eh? It was true. The king's face wore a decidedly crafty expression. He said nothing.

Leroy Williams repeated his question and yet still the old king refused to speak. At the third time of asking, Judge Wigmore was forced to intervene. Firmly but politely, she explained to King Edward that he was remembered by history as a good, honest and religious man. Would he like to lose that reputation?

No. Edward said that his reputation was the jewel in his crown. To lose it would be utterly dreadful.

Well, the judge advised, he should answer the questions put to him immediately and honestly. Looking very agitated, the king agreed to do as he was told.

'I will ask my question again, then,' said Leroy Williams when the judge had finished her ticking off. 'Sire, please tell the court to whom you offered the crown of England.'

What happened next was one of the most extraordinary scenes ever witnessed in the High Court of History. Edward the Confessor glanced over at William the Conqueror, then at the judge, then at the jury, and finally back at Leroy Williams. He raised his hands to the ceiling, tears spurted from his eyes and he burst out in a high-pitched wail: 'Woe! Woe is me! Help me Lord, for I have sinned!'

The court sat in open-mouthed astonishment, not knowing quite what to do as the king fell

to his knees, sobbing painfully. Leroy Williams walked over to the judge who whispered something in his ear. The lawyer nodded and returned to his desk. Five minutes later, the crying gradually faded away and King Edward rose slowly to his feet.

'I am ready to confess,' he said in a sad, low voice. 'I am a weak man. When things got tough, I didn't know what to do. I just said what I thought people wanted to hear.'

'And what was that?'

'I told Cnut's grandson that he could inherit my throne.'

'What?' gasped the defence lawyer. 'But I thought you told William of Normandy that he could inherit your throne?'

'I did,' said the king, looking as if he were about to burst into tears again. 'And then I said the same thing to Harold! Three men, all deceived by my evil tongue.'

'Deceived? Why deceived, sire?'

'Because the true heir to my throne was the boy, Edgar the Atheling. There, now you know the whole truth. It was all my fault, the invasions, the bloodshed, the bullying – just because I was not strong enough to stand up for what I knew to be right. I am to blame.'

As the old, snivelling king was led away before a stunned court, Leroy Williams turned to the jury. 'So there we have it. William the Conqueror, like Harold, was simply doing what he thought he had a right to do – take the crown that Edward had offered him.

'Therefore, ladies, gentlemen and children of the jury, I trust you will agree with me that on the charge of theft, William the Conqueror is not guilty!'

When Leroy Williams had sat down, Judge Wigmore reminded the jury that it was their job to reach a verdict. Miss Bessant, Mr Williams and

the witnesses had given them plenty of evidence. They must take their time, think carefully and be prepared to change their minds.

'And remember,' the judge concluded, 'that if you find William the Conqueror not guilty, he will be free to live out the rest of his second life in peace. But if you find him guilty, he will spend all his earthly days in prison.

'I now ask you to retire from the court and begin your deliberations.'

Dear Reader,

YOU are a member of the jury!

You were one of the two children sitting behind Jasmine and Tom.

If you go to my website **www.stewartross.com**, you can get in touch and tell me your decision: William the Conqueror, guilty or not guilty of stealing the throne of England?

I will write back and let you know how others have voted. And when we have enough votes, I'll put a page on my website announcing the verdict: William the Conqueror, guilty or innocent?

I do hope you enjoyed the book. If you did, you might like the others in the Timewarp Trials series.

Best wishes

1066 – the year of three Kings

1016	On the death of Ethelred the Unready, Cnut (Canute) seizes the throne of England.
1035	Cnut's son Harold Harefoot succeeds his father.
1040	Harthacnut, the second son King Cnut, comes to the throne on his brother's death.
1042	Harthacnut leaves the throne to Edward the Confessor, the eldest son of Ethelred the Unready. Edward is crowned King of England.
1051	Edward the Confessor promises his crown to William, Duke of Normandy.
c. 1064	Harold Godwineson goes to Normandy, perhaps to confirm King Edward's promise of the crown to

William. Harold swears an oath promising to help William to the crown on the death of Edward the Confessor.

1066   **5 January** Edward the Confessor dies after promising his crown to Harold Godwineson.

6 January Harold II crowned King of England with the support of all important people.

28 September William lands in England.

14 October Harold killed at the Battle of Hastings.

c. 16 October Londoners choose Edgar Atheling to be their King.

25 December William I (the Conqueror) crowned King of England in Westminster Abbey.

William the Conqueror and history

The crown of England

For hundreds of years, England was made up of
many small kingdoms, each with its own King.
By the year 959, these small kingdoms had come
together to make one big kingdom (England) ruled
by one King, Edgar.

After Edgar's death, there followed long years of
fighting and murder. Sometimes an Englishman
sat on the throne of England; at other times a
ruler from Denmark wore the crown. The most
successful, King Canute (also written Cnut, 1017-
1035), was Danish.

When Canute's two sons died young, the crown
of England went to an Englishman again. This
was Edward the Confessor (1042-1066). He had
no children, and when he died *three* men said they
should be the next King of England!

Three-way split

The three men who claimed the English crown were: (1) the King of Norway; (2) Earl Harold of England, whose sister had married Edward the Confessor; and (3) Duke William of Normandy, in France.

The situation was *even more* complicated because, at different times, Edward promised his crown to both Earl Harold *and* Duke William!

There was a traditional way of sorting out this muddle. A King was not crowned until he had been approved by a group of wise men known as the Witan. Immediately after Edward's death, Witan chose Earl Harold as their new king.

That should have been that. But it wasn't. William announced that, a few years earlier, Earl Harold had promised to help him get the English crown when Edward died...

History, the search for truth

Neither of the two lawyers in this book – Tanka Bessant and Leroy Williams – tell lies. They both argue using historical facts: William was Duke of Normandy, Harold was King of England, and William did invade England, kill Harold and take his crown.

But history is not just knowing facts; it's about deciding how important they are and what they mean. For example, when a king or queen dies in Britain nowadays, there are clear rules about who will take over from them; but back in the time of William the Conqueror there were no such rules.

Life in the past was different

So, what do we make of Duke William taking Harold's crown? He behaved violently and he was not the choice of the people of England. But, as Leroy Williams asks, was that a crime? People had been fighting to get their hands on the crown for hundreds of years. William was doing no more than many others had done before him.

We need to guard against believing people who lived 1,000 years ago thought as we do. If we want to judge them, we must first understand the very, very different times in which they lived. That's what makes the study of history so fascinating.

Glossary

Abbey:
Church run by monks or nuns

Awning:
Large covering or sunshade made of cloth or canvas

Confess:
Admit to doing wrong

Conquer:
Take over a land by force

Defendant:
Person in court accused of a crime

Dock:
Place in a courtroom where the accused person stands or sits

Foreman:
Leader of a jury who announces its innocent or guilty verdict

Heir:
Person who takes over (inherits) the possessions and sometimes the job of someone who has died

Invade:
Attack a land with an army

Juror:
Member of a jury

Jury:
Group who decide whether an accused person is innocent or guilty

Monk:
Man who does not marry and devotes his life to the service of God

Nun:
Female monk

Oath:
Promise made before God

Prosecutor:
Lawyer whose job is to prove to the jury that an accused person is guilty

Tapestry:
Image made by weaving coloured threads onto a cloth background

Venomous:
Poisonous

Verdict:
Decision in a law court – innocent or guilty

Wessex:
South-west England

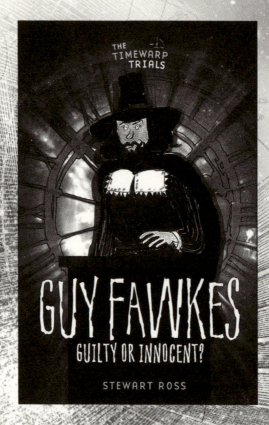